I0164385

Justification by Faith

Orientating the Church's teaching and practice to Christ

A lecture in honour of the Revd Dr Peter Toon

by Michael Nazir-Ali

The Latimer Trust

Justification by Faith: Orientating the Church's teaching and practice to Christ © Michael Nazir-Ali 2013

ISBN   978-1-906327-15-6

Cover photo: © Vita and Deborah Toon

Published by the Latimer Trust September 2013

The Latimer Trust (formerly Latimer House, Oxford) is a conservative Evangelical research organisation within the Church of England, whose main aim is to promote the history and theology of Anglicanism as understood by those in the Reformed tradition. Interested readers are welcome to consult its website for further details of its many activities.

The Latimer Trust
London N14 4PS UK
Registered Charity: 1084337
Company Number: 4104465
Web: www.latimertrust.org
E-mail: administrator@latimertrust.org

Views expressed in works published by The Latimer Trust are those of the authors and do not necessarily represent the official position of The Latimer Trust.

CONTENTS

Introduction

Peter Toon was a Yorkshireman, an Anglican clergyman, theologian, and church historian. Former librarian of Latimer House in Oxford, curate of St Ebbe's, and later a tutor at Oak Hill, after a brief spell in County Durham he was invited to become Professor of Philosophical and Systematic Theology at an Episcopal Seminary in Wisconsin, and served churches in the United States until almost the end of his life. He was for many years the President of the Prayer Book Society in the United States, but eventually returned to England to serve as Priest-in-Charge of a Staffordshire village church. He was widely in demand as a speaker throughout the Commonwealth, Europe, and Asia.

Dr. Toon died in April 2009. He left behind around 40 books and numerous essays and articles on a wide variety of topics from Puritanism and popular doctrinal works, to spirituality and liturgy. As well as editing *The Concise Evangelical Dictionary of Theology* and *The Compact Bible Dictionary*, he wrote on the great Puritan, John Owen, publishing his *Oxford Orations*, his surviving correspondence, and a biography, *God's Statesman*. But the burden of much of Peter Toon's writing was for the importance of the historic formularies of the Church of England: the *Thirty-nine Articles*, the *Book of Common Prayer*, and the Ordinal.

He also left his beloved wife of more than 48 years, Vita, and their daughter, Deborah, and it is with their help that a new annual lectureship – the Peter Toon Lecture – has been established, in the hope that it will contribute to the strengthening of God's church, and particularly the Reformed Catholic faith of the Church of England.

The inaugural Toon Lecture on 16th April 2013 was preceded, appropriately, by Evening Prayer in the chapel at Wycliffe Hall, Oxford. It was led by Canon David Wheaton, former Principal of Oak Hill Theological College, with involvement from several others including the preacher, Revd Lee Gatiss, Director of Church Society, who had organised the occasion.

Before the lecture, as a special honour to Vita Toon who had travelled all the way from California for the event, Alistair Macdonald-Radcliff made a special presentation to her on behalf of the Prayer Book Society USA. In Peter's honour, and at the suggestion of Dr Ashley Null, they had paid for the refurbishment and repair of one of Thomas

Cranmer's own library books (his copy of Primasius' commentary on Revelation, from 1544) and so presented her with a copy of the title page of this rare volume, alongside a special inscription.

The inaugural lecture itself was delivered by Bishop Michael Nazir-Ali, former bishop of Rochester. A personal friend of Peter and Vita Toon, Dr. Nazir-Ali is of course no stranger to Oxford, to Reformed Catholicism, and to controversy. His latest book *Triple Jeopardy for the West* examines the very hot topics of aggressive secularism, radical Islam, and multiculturalism. He is currently the President of the Oxford Centre for Training, Research, Advocacy, and Dialogue, and his subject for the lecture was what the *Thirty-nine Articles* call the "most wholesome doctrine" of justification by faith.

In a tour-de-force, Bishop Michael tackled the subject exegetically, historically, theologically, and pastorally. It was stretching, though intelligible for the ordinary lay Christian, and demonstrated good evidence of keeping up with contemporary scholarship on this subject, which is of course vast. The packed lecture room at Wycliffe Hall (standing room only!) greatly enjoyed his thoughtful, earnest, yet also occasionally witty presentation which ranged widely from Genesis 15 and Galatians 3, to Augustine, the Reformers, the Council of Trent, Tom Wright, John Piper, and Benedict XVI.

There were a significant number of younger people and those who had never met Dr. Toon personally who came, as well as friends, family, and former colleagues. Interest in the Anglican Reformed tradition, which Peter Toon expounded so well in his writings, is alive and well in the next generation. It is greatly to be hoped that this new endeavour will serve them well, far into the future, that they may be confident and equipped to defend and promote the theology of grace, for the glory of God and the good of his kingdom.

Lee Gatiss
Cambridge

Justification by Faith: Orientating the Church's teaching and practice to Christ.

A lecture in honour of the Revd Dr Peter Toon

Justification in the Bible

In his influential and comparative work *The Christian Understanding of Atonement*, the Oxford scholar, F. W. Dillistone, has noted the idea of an original universal harmony which is found within many cultures and religious traditions. This harmony, moreover, is often seen to have been disrupted and must be put right through some kind of cosmic or eternal sacrifice. The sacrificial rituals of different civilisations, which he examines in some detail, attempt to portray and to participate in such a sacrifice. By the offering of a sacrificial victim, those who offer the sacrifice become involved in the business of cosmic death and renewal. Dillistone allows that in many ancient cultures such rituals had become cults of 'dying and rising gods' closely associated with the cycle of nature and the fertility both of the earth and of human beings.[1]

When we come to the Bible, we enter a different world altogether. It is true that the ideas of life renewal and life enhancement are present in the Jewish sacrificial cultus, but the emphasis is very much either on celebrating God's mighty acts of deliverance – we might say God putting right the injustice and the oppression suffered by his people – or on the expiation of sin. As far as the latter is concerned, the terms often used for the sacrifices, e.g. אשם and חטאת also stand for the sins for which the sacrifices are being offered. What is important here to note is that notions of a sacrifice 'representing' and 'substituting' for the offerer are already to the fore – and without these it would be difficult to make sense of the Bible's provision of sacrifice.[2] By the

---

[1]   F.W. Dillistone, *The Christian Understanding of Atonement* (Welwyn: Nisbet, 1968), pp 29ff.

[2]   See Michael Nazir-Ali, *The Unique and Universal Christ: Jesus in a Plural World* (Milton Keynes: Paternoster Press, 2008), pp 45ff and R. J. Thompson's article on 'Sacrifice in the Old Testament' in *The Illustrated Bible Dictionary* (Leicester: IVP, 1980), vol 3, pp 1358ff.

offering of the victim, the person or the community is, in some sense, being put right by God.

The system of sacrifice is to be understood then in the wider background of the just God who wills justice in the world which he has created. This justice has been disrupted by human wilfulness and rebellion and needs to be restored. The notion of animal and other sacrifices was, however, the subject of a severe critique by the prophets who saw an over-reliance on its mechanical observance as obscuring the necessity for a change of heart and need to honour God with the whole of our lives. The former Chief Rabbi, Lord Jakobovits, has pointed out that the writing prophets are not wanting to do away with sacrifice altogether but to emphasise, rather, its spiritual and moral aspect. It is this which leads them, and the Psalmist, to exalt self-sacrifice over and against mere ritual as a surer way of restoring a relationship with God.[3]

There is also a growing recognition in the Old Testament that the suffering of representative people, prophets and martyrs, for example, can and does lead to the fulfilment of God's saving purposes. The theme of the Son of Man in Daniel and of the Suffering Servant in Isaiah show how a representative figure recapitulates in himself both the suffering of God's people as well as their vindication by God. All of this is brought to a head in Psalm 40 where a representative figure steps forward in obedience and this brings about communal deliverance. The writer of the Letter to the Hebrews, in his commentary on this passage, encapsulates the entire purpose of the sacrificial system and sees in the coming of Jesus the fulfilment of the hope for a messianic figure who, by his work of suffering for the people, finds vindication by God. By his freely-willed obedience, the eternal and incarnate Son offers up himself as a final, unrepeatable and unique sacrifice: as so often in the Bible, the speculation, myths, and wistful longings of humanity are brought to the bar of a historical event, a person in whom God is himself acting in a saving and sacrificial way (Psalm 40:6-8, cf. Hebrews 10:5-7).[4]

As Peter Toon pointed out in his Justification and Sanctification, the keywords here are the Hebrew צדק and the Greek δικαιοω. According to him, in the Old Testament the term has a forensic meaning i.e. the verdict of a judge in favour of one party, thus declaring it to be just or

---

[3] Immanuel Jakobovits in *The Authorised Daily Prayer Book* (St Ives: Singers, 1992), pp 918ff.
[4] Nazir-Ali, *The Unique and Universal Christ*, pp 46ff.

righteous. But this also carries ethical overtones, meaning that someone has remained within the covenant of faith. The key to understanding the meaning of צדק is to think of relationships and their right ordering whether with God, the very source of our being, our fellow human beings or, indeed, with the natural world. The Hebrew, as the Arabic today, also has the sense of personal integrity or character. The story of the Old Testament, however, is that of God's faithfulness but also of the faithlessness of humans, even of his chosen people. So how is God's 'saving justice' to come about? One answer in the Old Testament is that it will come about through the Messianic King who will bring God's justice to the world, freeing people from oppression and bringing prosperity to them (Psalm 72:1-4, Psalm 146:7-9).

The words related to δικαιοω in the New Testament, in spite of their etymology, certainly have a declarative intent: not then so much to make righteous as to declare righteous. And yet, as John Piper points out in his response to Tom Wright, such a declaration also accomplishes something. He takes Romans 5:1 as his point of departure: "Therefore, since we have been justified by faith, we have peace with God through our Lord Jesus Christ." That it is to say, alongside God's calling and the awakening of faith, God does something which makes that person's standing right with God. Such a declaration of acquittal, on the basis of faith, which unites us with Christ, also makes us members of his body and thus of the covenant community.[5]

In this way, we become part of God's-single-plan-through-Israel-for-the-world, as Tom Wright has pointed out, and which has long been understood by biblical theologians as the meaning of Salvation History.[6] The big picture, important as it is, should not though crowd out the personal. Membership of the covenant community must hinge on the individual's God-given faith that his or her sins have been dealt with by Christ standing in his or her place and by Christ's faithfulness, even bearing the ultimate punishment for sin *viz.* death, thus averting God's anger from the sins of the individual. My sin and his and hers is no longer reckoned or imputed to us but the righteousness of the obedient Christ is. He, as our representative head and sacrificial substitute,

---

[5] John Piper, *The Future of Justification: A Response to N T Wright* (Nottingham: IVP, 2008), pp 40ff.

[6] N. T. Wright, *Justification: God's Plan and Paul's Vision* (London: SPCK 2009), pp 18f, 212f etc.

reconciles us to God, thus ending the enmity (2 Corinthians 5:19, 20; Ephesians 2:15, 16). The all-important word here is λογίζομαι and its cognates in Romans 4 and Galatians 3:6 (the usage in James 2:23 is, admittedly, somewhat different): Abraham had faith in God and it was *reckoned* (or *imputed*) to him as righteousness (cf. Genesis 15:6 where a cognate of צדק is, in fact, used). What is true of Abraham the father of the faithful, must also be true of every believer. We must then, along with St Paul, insist on the justification and forgiveness of all those in Christ without forgetting that each one of us has to be justified and forgiven. It is not enough to say that we are part of the corporate body. The Bible is full of people, in both the Old and New Testaments, who claimed such membership but who could not be 'reckoned' righteous as Abraham was.

Both Tom Wright and his opponents agree that in Ephesians, the two (or several?) perspectives come together: if Ephesians 2:1-10 is about sinners saved by grace through faith, the rest of the chapter is about the breaking down of the dividing wall of hostility between Jews and Gentiles. We might add, for good measure, that chapters 1 and 3 reveal to us God's cosmic plan 'to unite all things in Christ, things in heaven and on earth (1:10).[7]

Justification in Church History

In the Anglican tradition, there have been those, like Richard Hooker, who have attempted to understand justification in ecclesiological terms, for example, in seeing baptism as the sacrament of justifying righteousness and the Lord's Supper as the sacrament of sanctification (the sacraments being, as it were, the external forum for inward grace).[8] Equally, there have been others, such as J. C. Ryle, the first Bishop of Liverpool, who have emphasised, rather, the individual in the transaction that takes place. For Ryle, justification is the *counting* of a person to be righteous because of what Jesus Christ has done, whereas sanctification is *making* a person righteous. The first righteousness is not ours but is Christ's and is perfect; the second, which is imparted to us by the Holy Spirit is ours but it is imperfect. The first is always complete whereas in the second there is room for growth – indeed,

---

[7] Wright, *Justification*, pp 144, 150f.

[8] Peter Toon, *Justification and Sanctification* (London: Marshall, Morgan & Scott, 1983), pp 94f.

there must be growth until the resurrection. In holding such a view, although differing in emphasis, Ryle's position is not all that different from the one set out in Hookers' famous sermon *A Learned Discourse of Justification.*

Against this, however, there developed another view, characterised by some of the so-called Caroline divines of the 17th century, that although justification was made possible for us by the righteousness of Christ, it was made actual by our faith which God accepted as the basis of our justification. (It was said that Abraham *believed* God and it was counted to him for righteousness Genesis 15:6 and related verses in the New Testament). Such faith, for them, is not merely believing (which even demons do – James 2:19) but actively trusting in God, resulting in a new attitude and good works which flow from this. These Caroline divines, clearly, were trying to meet the dangers of antinomianism but the question arises 'faith in what?' Can it not be fairly said that it must be in what Christ, our leader, representative, substitute and head, has done so that we may be acceptable because of our own union with him? Of course, it can be said that a changed attitude and good works are a sign that we have been justified but justification cannot be made to depend on them or even on faith itself but, rather, on God's grace given in what Christ has done for us.[9] This does not mean that we have to know what a correct doctrine of justification is but it must mean that we accept that forgiveness of sins is through who Jesus is and what he has done (Acts 13:38,39).

From the earliest period, there has been debate about how the initial event of justification relates to the growing sanctification of the believer. St Augustine of Hippo is quoted on every side of the matter and whether he believed in the imputation of Christ's righteousness to the believer or no, he certainly believed that it is the righteousness of God alone brought to us through Christ which avails for salvation. For Augustine, however, and for the whole of the Latin tradition after him, *justificare* tended to mean 'to make righteous' and so justification was seen not simply as an event but as a process by which we increase in holiness and love.[10] The passage often quoted here, Galatians 5:6, 'faith working through love', became an important point of debate and polemics at the time of the Reformation. The Reformers, relying on

---

[9]   Toon, *Justification and Sanctification,* 97f.

[10]   Toon, *Justification and Sanctification,* pp 45f.

Erasmus' edition of the Greek Testament and its Latin translation, taught that faith was primary and love its necessary result against mediaeval attempts to make the verse mean that is was our love that brought about faith.[11] How far we have come, partly because of biblical scholarship, is shown by Pope Benedict, in his work *Paul of Tarsus*, where he translates the passage as 'faith that works through love' in a way that the Reformation-minded would have approved.[12]

As the Anglican-Roman Catholic agreement, *Salvation and the Church*, recognises:-

> "The theologians of the Reformation tended to follow the predominant usage of the New Testament, in which the verb *dikaioun* usually means to 'pronounce righteous.' The Catholic theologians, and notably the Council of Trent, tended to follow the usage of patristic and medieval Latin writers, for whom *justificare* (the traditional translation of *dikaioun*) signified 'to make righteous.' Thus the Catholic understanding of the process of justification, following Latin usage, tended to include elements of salvation which the Reformers would describe as belonging to sanctification rather than justification. As a consequence, Protestants took Catholics to be emphasising sanctification in such a way that the absolute gratuitousness of salvation was threatened. On the other side, Catholics feared that Protestants were so stressing the justifying action of God that sanctification and human responsibility were gravely depreciated."[13]

The Reformers certainly held that we were counted right with God because of Christ's obedience being imputed to us. This 'justifying righteousness' is not ours, it is alien to us, but is given to us as a gracious gift. It results in a work of the Holy Spirit which brings about a righteousness which is ours. The former is perfect as Hooker saw, whilst the latter, in this life at any rate, is imperfect. This means, among other things, that the justified believer is *simul justus et peccator* (at the same time righteous and a sinner). This teaching was seen as denied by

---

[11]   See, for example, William Tyndale's invective against the Bishop of Rochester, John Fisher, in *The Obedience of the Christian Man* (London: Penguin, 2000), pp 8of.

[12]   Benedict XVI, *Paul of Tarsus* (London: Catholic Truth Society, 2009), p 101.

[13]   *Salvation and the Church* (London: Catholic Truth Society and Anglican Consultative Council, 1987), p 17.

the Council of Trent amongst its prominent apologists. The imparting or infusion of Christ's righteousness, which was regarded as the single formal cause of justification, was such that it expelled all sin in its true nature and character. Any lapse from such post-baptismal purity could only be treated through the sacrament of penance which would restore the Christian to purity.[14]

Peter Toon has pointed out that even in the heat of controversy at the Reformation, agreement on this matter was possible between the Reformers and at least some Catholic theologians. To illustrate the extent of what was even then possible, he published Article 5 of the Regensburg Agreement of 1541 which spoke of justification in terms of 'righteousness which is imputed to us on account of Christ and his merit, not on account of the worthiness or perfection of the righteousness imparted to us in Christ.'[15] At Trent also, there were those, like Cardinal Pole, the Englishman, later to be Papal Legate and Archbishop of Canterbury under Mary Tudor, and Cardinal Seripando, the head of the Augustinians, who wanted to maintain a position which would have permitted imperfection and the existence of sin in the justified believer but their views did not prevail. The Anglican Newman too had insisted on the presence of Christ in us, in addition to inherent righteousness, as that which makes us right with God.[16]

Hans Kung, in his work *Justification* claims that the Liturgy of the Roman Catholic Church, since Trent, assumes believers to be *simul justus et peccator. Salvation and the Church* notes that *Lumen Gentium*, the Dogmatic Constitution on the Church, of the Second Vatican Council, states that the Church is at once holy and in need of purification, constantly following the path of penance and renewal.[17] This seems to echo Karl Rahner's teaching that the Church is sinful both as a matter of doctrine and of experience. The Lutheran-Roman Catholic agreement on justification claims that Lutheran and Catholic views of the remaining sinfulness of believers can be expressed in *simul justus et peccator* language in spite of the differences between Trent

---

[14] C. Fitzsimmons Allison, *The Pastoral and Biblical Implications of Trent on Justification* (Sewanee, TN: School of Theology, University of the South, 1988).
[15] Peter Toon in *Justification and Sanctification*, p 88f and 105f.
[16] Allison, *Pastoral and Biblical Implications of Trent.*
[17] Lumen Gentium 8 in A. Flannery (ed.), *Vatican Council II, The Conciliar and Post Conciliar Documents* (New York: Costello), 1988, p 358, and Salvation to the Church, p 21.

and the Lutheran confessions.[18] *Salvation and the Church* similarly uses the expression, pointing out that it is of Augustinian inspiration.[19] If all of this means that sinners are justified by the righteousness of Christ alone and that any imparted righteousness remains imperfect and coexists with sinfulness (however that is understood), then this is to be welcomed so long as there is no ambiguity. As Toon remarks, in his exposition of the work of Michael Schmaus, a Roman Catholic theologian, it would have been better, for all concerned, if Trent had been able to distinguish between justification and sanctification.[20]

The great Reformation Confessions repeatedly affirm that justification comes about through faith alone – *ex sola fide Jesu Christi* and we are accounted just before God *propter meritum Domini* (by the merit of the Lord). However, although we are justified by faith alone, faith is never alone for it is always accompanied by love and operates through love. Good works are the necessary fruit of faith and reveal its genuineness. Here there has been an unusual intervention: Pope Benedict in his addresses *Paul of Tarsus* tells us that, for St Paul, after his conversion, saving justice through faith in Jesus Christ became a dominant theme that runs through his letters. Referring to Romans 3:23-24, he repeats that all have sinned and fallen short of the glory of God and are now justified by grace as a gift, through the redemption which is in Christ. In going on to Romans 3:28, he tells us that though the text reads: "We hold that a man is justified by faith apart from works", Luther translated this as "justified by faith alone", even if 'alone' is not in the text. He goes on to say, remarkably, and against the thrust of much post-Reformation Roman Catholic exegesis, that Luther was correct in doing this as it is Christ who makes us just, further observances are unnecessary. Later on, he goes on to explore the relationship between faith and love in ways to which even Tyndale could not have taken exception![21] The Lutheran-Roman Catholic joint declaration states that "the doctrine of justification is that measure or touchstone for the Christian faith. No teaching may contradict this criterion. In this sense, the doctrine of justification is "an indispensable criterion that consistently serves to orient all the teaching and practice

---

[18] *Joint Declaration on the Doctrine of Justification* (Grand Rapids: Eerdmans, 2000), p 44.
[19] Salvation and the Church, in Flannery, *Vatican Council II*, p21.
[20] Toon, *Justification and Sanctification*, p 122.
[21] Benedict XVI, *Paul of Tarsus*, pp 98ff.

of our churches to Christ."[22]   Would that the Council of Trent had listened to those Protestants who attended some of its sessions! We would certainly have been spared much division and suffering. This is not to say that what Hooker called the 'grand question' that hangs between Rome and the Reformation has been resolved. Toon himself points to a whole host of remaining issues but, because of the renewal of biblical scholarship, perhaps, the rules about the discussion have changed and some Catholics are at least willing to consider the issues raised by the Reformers.

The Joint Declaration tackles head on the question of assurance; we should look away from our own weakness, as the Reformers taught, and look only to Christ and trust solely in him. It is constantly by looking to Christ that we are preserved in grace.[23]   As a result of the debate between John Piper and Tom Wright, it is important to reiterate that our final justification is as much a matter of our faith in Christ as our initial justification. The works produced by the sanctifying work of the Holy Spirit are, to be sure, signs and tokens that we have been justified by faith in all that Jesus has done for us but they should not be taken, in any way, as contributing to our final justification. To do this would be to unravel the whole force of the Reformation view that we are saved by trusting in what God has done for us rather than our own efforts.[24]

Justification Today

One of the criticisms of the doctrine of justification has been that it is well-nigh impossible to make it intelligible to present day society, at least in the Western world.[25]   One of the ways in which we can begin to communicate this essential doctrine is to point to the experienced alienation of modern human beings: from others, from their work, even from themselves and, ultimately, from the very source and ground of their being, God. Another aspect of contemporary life is anxiety: there is a crisis about existence itself; its fragility and its meaning. There is also

---

[22]   *Joint Declaration on the Doctrine of Justification*, pp 46f.
[23]   *Joint Declaration on the Doctrine of Justification*, pp 23f, 35f.
[24]   John Piper, *The Future of Justification: A Response to N.T. Wright*, pp 117ff.
[25]   Toon, *Justification and Sanctification*, pp 126f. Paul Tillich, *New Being* (New York: Scribner, 1955) and *Systematic Theology* vol 3 (Chicago: University of Chicago Press, 1976).

a sense of guilt about our past in what has gone wrong: the betrayals, the deceptions and self-deceptions, the misuse of power, the wrong acquisition of wealth, and so much else. People are fearful about the state of the world, the threat of war, the breakdown of family and of civil society, radical environmental degradation, and nuclear holocaust.

In order to mask the loneliness and the anxiety, men, women, and even children have given themselves over to addictions of various sorts: endless entertainment, consumerism, drugs, alcohol, and pornography. They seek refuge in these from the stresses and strains of life but, of course, these addictions produce new problems of health, of relationships, or mental well-being.

In such a context, the Gospel of being forgiven because of what Christ has done for us, of being accepted and pronounced to be right with God can lead to the reunification of divided personalities, the renewal of relationships, the freeing from anxiety about our immediate or ultimate fate, in short to what the Bible calls the fruit of the Spirit (Galatians 5:22f). We are rescued from our constant need to hide our fears and to live with our heads held high because we have been declared to be God's children through the grace of adoption (Romans 8:12-17, Galatians 4:6-7). Such a realisation of acceptance, of true freedom, of being part of God's covenant people, throughout history and across the world, and of a personal relationship with Christ as the friend who is always for us can make a proclamation of justification by grace and through faith just what is needed today.

Peter Toon comments that Paul's teaching on justification by faith, hammered out in the context of Jesus' own critique of works-oriented religion, came to life at the time of the Reformation as the Reformers confronted a distortion of the Gospel by an over-reliance on works.[26]

As I have experienced, and as Peter and Vita no doubt saw when they visited us, Paul's teaching on justification also comes alive in the context of Islamist revivalism with its emphasis on strict enforcement of the *Shar'ia*, on minute rules for daily living and on ritual prayer etc. To understand, in such a situation, that we are accepted by God not because of what we are able to do, which is always radically inadequate, but because of what Christ has done for us is, indeed, to be liberated

---

[26] Toon, *Justification and Sanctification*, pp 135ff.

from the law of sin and death and to find ourselves free children of the promise. In both mission and in teaching, this doctrine then remains at the fore and at the core of our identity as Christians and of the Church's identity as the Bride of Christ who is made perfect by and for the Bridegroom.

+Michael Nazir-Ali

The Writings of Peter Toon

With thanks to David Virtue of VirtueOnline (http://www.virtueonline.org), here is a list of Peter Toon's major publications.

His first piece appeared in *The Baptist Quarterly* (a publication of the Baptist Union of Great Britain) on the topic of 'The Strict and Particular Baptists' in 1963 when he was studying for the B.D. at King's College, University of London.

His first book continued the theme of 'Calvinism' and appeared in 1967 as *The Emergence of Hyper-Calvinism in English Nonconformity, 1689-1765*. It has a Preface by Dr. J. I. Packer and it was the cause of various invitations to the author to lecture in the U.S.A.

Then, in general categories, his works may be listed thus:

On English Puritanism
The Emergence of Hyper-Calvinism (1967)
The Correspondence of John Owen (1970)
Puritans the Millennium (1970)
Puritans and Calvinism (1971)
God's Statesman (1972)
The University Orations of Dr John Owen (1973)

Semi-Popular Doctrinal Writings
El Dios Siempre Presente
The Right of Private Judgment (1975)
Jesus Christ is Lord (1978)
Free to Obey (1979)
God Here and Now (1979)
God's Church for Today (1980)
God's Kingdom for Today (1980)
God's Salvation for Today (1980)
Protestant and Catholic (1983)
What's the Difference? (1983)
What We Believe (1984)
Your Conscience as Your Guide (1984)
General Godliness and True Piety (2000)

Serious Doctrinal Writing
Justification and Sanctification (1983)
The Ascension of our Lord (1984)
Heaven and Hell (1986)
The End of Liberal Theology (1995)

Yesterday, Today and Forever (1996)
Our Triune God (1996 & 2002)

On Spirituality
About Turn: the Decisional Event of Conversion (1987)
Born Again (1987)
What is Spirituality? (1989)
Spiritual Companions (100?)

Meditation
From Mind to Heart (1987)
Longing for Heaven (1987)
Meditating as a Christian (1991)
The Art of Meditating on Scripture (1993)
Meditating Upon God's Word (1998)

On Anglican Theology and Liturgy
The Ordinal and its Revision (1974)
The Development of Doctrine in the Church (1979)
Evangelical Theology 1833-1856 (1979)
The Anglican Way, Evangelical and Catholic (1983)
Britain's True Greatness (1984)
Let Women be Women (1990)
Knowing God through the Liturgy (1992)
Proclaiming the Gospel through the Liturgy (1993)
Which Rite is Right? (1994)
Common Worship Considered (2003)
Reforming Forwards? (2003)
The Order for Evening Prayer (1662) Annotated (2004)
The Order for Holy Communion (1662) Annotated (2004)
The Order for Holy Communion (1928) Annotated (2004)
Same-Sex Affection, Holiness and Ordination (2005)
Worship Without Dumbing Down (2005)
The Anglican Formularies and Holy Scripture (2006)
Anglican Identity (2006)
Episcopal Innovations 1960-2004 in ECUSA (2006)
Mystical Washing and Spiritual Regeneration (2007)
On Salvation and the Church of Rome – Richard Hooker (2007)

Writings in cooperation with Lou Tarsitano, edited by Toon
The Way, The Truth and the Life: The Anglican Walk (1998)
Dear Primates (2000)
Neither Archaic nor Obsolete (2003)
Neither Orthodoxy nor a Formulary (2004)

Essays with others in Books edited by Toon wholly or partly
Puritans, the Millennium and the Future of Israel (1970)

John Charles Ryle, Evangelical Bishop (1976)
One God in Trinity (1980)
Real Questions (with David Field, 1982)
Let God be God (1990)
A Guidebook to the Spiritual Life (1998)

Individual Essays in Books edited by others
"Anglicanism in Popish Dress," in *Tradition Renewed* (1986)
"Appreciating Mary Today" in *Chosen by God, Mary* (1989)
"The Articles and Homilies" in *The Study of Anglicanism* (1998)
Chaps 2 & 3 in *To Mend the Net* (2001)
"Episcopalianism" in *Who Runs The Church?* (2004)
"Justification by Faith Alone" in *Justification and Sanctification* (Canada 2008)

Dictionaries as an Editor
The Compact Bible Dictionary (1987)
NIV Bible Guide (1987)
The Concise Dictionary of the Christian Tradition (1989)
The Concise Evangelical Dictionary of Theology (1992)

Prayer Books as primary editor
Worshipping the Lord in the Anglican Way (2004)
An Anglican Prayer Book (2008)

Classic short works on the Devotional Life as editor
St Francis de Sales, Introduction to the Devout Life (1988)
Christ for All Seasons, Thomas a Kempis (1989)
Benjamin Jenks, Prayers for Families (1990)

Magazines edited by the author
HOME WORDS, Parish magazine insert C of E, 1985-
MANDATE, Prayer Book Society Magazine, USA, 1995-2008

If you have enjoyed this book, you might like to consider

- *supporting the work of the Latimer Trust*
- *reading more of our publications*
- *recommending them to others*

See www.latimertrust.org for more information.

Latimer Publications

Latimer Publications

LB05	Christ's Gospel to the Nations: The Heart & Mind of Evangelicalism Past, Present & Future	Peter Jensen
LB06	Passion for the Gospel: Hugh Latimer (1485–1555) Then and Now. A commemorative lecture to mark the 450th anniversary of his martyrdom in Oxford	A. McGrath
LB07	Truth and Unity in Christian Fellowship	Michael Nazir-Ali
LB08	Unworthy Ministers: Donatism and Discipline Today	Mark Burkill
LB09	Witnessing to Western Muslims: A Worldview Approach to Sharing Faith	Richard Shumack
LB10	Scarf or Stole at Ordination? A Plea for the Evangelical Conscience	Andrew Atherstone
LB11	How to Write a Theology Essay	Michael P. Jensen
LB12	Preaching: A Guidebook for Beginners	Allan Chapple
LB13	Justification by Faith: Orientating the Church's teaching and practice to Christ (Toon Lecture 1)	Michael Nazir-Ali

Latimer Books

GGC	God, Gays and the Church: Human Sexuality and Experience in Christian Thinking	eds. Lisa Nolland, Chris Sugden, Sarah Finch
WTL	The Way, the Truth and the Life: Theological Resources for a Pilgrimage to a Global Anglican Future	eds. Vinay Samuel, Chris Sugden, Sarah Finch
AEID	Anglican Evangelical Identity – Yesterday and Today	J.I.Packer, N.T.Wright
IB	The Anglican Evangelical Doctrine of Infant Baptism	John Stott, Alec Motyer
BF	Being Faithful: The Shape of Historic Anglicanism Today	Theological Resource Group of GAFCON
TPG	The True Profession of the Gospel: Augustus Toplady and Reclaiming our Reformed Foundations	Lee Gatiss
SG	Shadow Gospel: Rowan Williams and the Anglican Communion Crisis	Charles Raven
TTB	Translating the Bible: From Willliam Tyndale to King James	Gerald Bray
PWS	Pilgrims, Warriors, and Servants: Puritan Wisdom for Today's Church	ed. Lee Gatiss
PPA	Preachers, Pastors, and Ambassadors: Puritan Wisdom for Today's Church	ed. Lee Gatiss
CWP	The Church, Women Bishops and Provision: The Integrity of Orthodox Objections to the Proposed Legislation Allowing Women Bishops	

Anglican Foundations Series

FWC	The Faith We Confess: An Exposition of the 39 Articles	Gerald Bray
AF02	The 'Very Pure Word of God': The Book of Common Prayer as a Model of Biblical Liturgy	Peter Adam
AF03	Dearly Beloved: Building God's People Through Morning and Evening Prayer	Mark Burkill
AF04	Day by Day: The Rhythm of the Bible in the Book of Common Prayer	Benjamin Sargent

www.ingramcontent.com/pod-product-compliance
Lightning Source LLC
Chambersburg PA
CBHW030014040426
42337CB00012BA/776